GW00976002

EMPOWERED
2022

WORDS UNBROKEN

Edited By Iain McQueen

First published in Great Britain in 2022 by:

Young Writers
Remus House
Coltsfoot Drive
Peterborough
PE2 9BF
Telephone: 01733 890066
Website: www.youngwriters.co.uk

All Rights Reserved
Book Design by Ashley Janson
© Copyright Contributors 2022
Softback ISBN 978-1-80459-059-1

Printed and bound in the UK by BookPrintingUK
Website: www.bookprintinguk.com
YB0509CZ

★ FOREWORD ★

Since 1991, here at Young Writers we have celebrated the awesome power of creative writing, especially in young adults where it can serve as a vital method of expressing their emotions and views about the world around them. In every poem we see the effort and thought that each student published in this book has put into their work and by creating this anthology we hope to encourage them further with the ultimate goal of sparking a life-long love of writing.

Our latest competition for secondary school students, Empowered, challenged young writers to consider what was important to them. We wanted to give them a voice, the chance to express themselves freely and honestly, something which is so important for these young adults to feel confident and listened to. They could give an opinion, share a memory, consider a dilemma, impart advice or simply write about something they love. There were no restrictions on style or subject so you will find an anthology brimming with a variety of poetic styles and topics. We hope you find it as absorbing as we have.

We encourage young writers to express themselves and address subjects that matter to them, which sometimes means writing about sensitive or contentious topics. If you have been affected by any issues raised in this book, details on where to find help can be found at www.youngwriters.co.uk/info/other/contact-lines

✭ CONTENTS ✭

Lymm High School, Lymm

Daisy Cook (16)	64
Harriet Dougall (14)	66
Noah Richardson (11)	67
Scarlett Gould (12)	68
Pia Mittag (13)	69
Alanna Baker (13)	70

Nottingham Girls' Academy, Aspley

Aliyah Bakhressa (13)	71
Zeeneth Araf (14)	72

The Aylesbury Vale Academy, Aylesbury

Julia Borucinska (11)	74
Chloe Evans (11)	75
Ellina Sarpong (12)	76
Alexandra Jordaan (12)	77

The FitzWimarc School, Rayleigh

Millie Trafford (12)	78
Grace King (11)	80
Mia Warwick (14)	81
Shannon Newby (11)	82
Freya Bourdon (13)	83
Olivia Wilkinson (11)	84
Sophie Attard (11)	85
Finn Tyrell (13)	86
Autumn Barteluk (11)	87
Rebecca Wilson (11)	88

The Link Secondary School, Beddington

Idris Yunus (15)	89
Niall McKelvey (17)	90
Alex Francis (13)	91
Aiden Mottram (15)	92

The Sacred Heart Language College, Wealdstone

Ksanette Samrai (11)	93
Coleen Moran (12)	94
Kitty Norrington (12)	96
Elishka Dodoo (14)	98
Mehwish Herwitker (11)	100
Maria Ottaviani (12)	101
Francene De Sa Pinto (11)	102
Olivie Dodoo (11)	103
Nelly Materka (11)	104
Lilly Chapman (12)	105
Marta Sadowska (11)	106
Dália Sequeira (13)	107
Olivia Seah (14)	108
Isabella Martinas (11)	109
Raissa Dos Reis Pereira (14)	110
Sanvi Vyas (14)	111
Georgia Gennaro (12)	112
Victoria Lubamba (14)	113
Maxime Dzogang (13)	114
Annabelle Do Rosario (11)	115
Lydia Daniel Semere (13)	116
Ashley Rose Seby (12)	117
Olivia Cummings (12)	118
Heba Hussain (13)	119
Odilia Figueiras (12)	120
April Tsangaris (13)	121
Neneh Dabo (12)	122
Chloe Caca (12)	123
Joanne Antony (13)	124
Zainab Tayab (12)	125
Giulia Cicu (12)	126
Noadiah Kennedy (14)	127
Natalia Gancarczyk (14)	128
Andrina Gomes (12)	129
Justyna Puterko (13)	130
Tobi Kadiri (13)	131
Thea Porter-German (13)	132
Precious Gbete (12)	133
Ahana Das (12)	134
Sienna Power (11)	135
Lujain Al Awad (12)	136

Melanie Shaikh (12)	137
Molly Carey (12)	138
Gabriella Cameron (11)	139
Victoria Damian (11)	140
Vishalini Ponnuthurai (11)	141
Rheya-Leigh Sturridge (11)	142
Natalie Hui (11)	143
Natalia Gancarczyk (14)	144
Kenechi Ezeajughi (13)	145
Anne Shelton (11)	146
Kate Gurhy (12)	147
Riana Antonia Petrisor (12)	148
Amy Flynn (12)	149
Kaitlyn Joyce (11)	150
Eugenie Malvezin (11)	151
Jade Montes (13)	152
Julia Kucia (12)	153
Colette Grant (11)	154
Raya Georgieva (11)	155
Tatiana Soares De Graca (12)	156
Vailanni Peixoto (11)	157

West Buckland School, Barnstaple

Zuzanna Filipczyk (11)	158
Emily Goddard (11)	159

THE POEMS

Focus

I sit when the quiet is gone.
I can hear the sound of the wind
Blowing in my hair.
The sound of kids having fun.
While to them, the hubbub is loud.
And not quite silence
The tree blows with leaves, saying bye to their home.
The smell of the fresh air is not repelling but sweet.
The blossoms bloom and rise from the ground.
Although I just sit on a hill in a field.
Still, joy is not kept.
And doesn't come to me.
Because, I, myself, am not satisfied by me, but other faces of joy.
It gets to me.
And I'm not saying I'm never happy.
But people bring me joy.
And at least the hubbub never stops, the wind still blows.
I'm okay.

Evie Sansom (12)
Aurora Eccles School, Eccles

Aurora Eccles

Aurora Eccles is an amazing place
It's a beautiful space to be
There is nice scenery
With lots of trees and greenery
Maintenance keeps the grounds neat
The cafeteria has lots of yummy things to eat
The pool is fun to swim and splash
We have a forest school that's pretty flash
Us kids like to play outside
But when it's cold, we're inside
The teachers are alright, I guess
They don't get cross if we make a mess
But we do sometimes make them stressed
Aurora Eccles is an amazing place.

Hayden Crow
Aurora Eccles School, Eccles

Divorce Force

When I was nine, my parents gave me a sign
That they might get a divorce, that really hurt me of course
I started to cry all day and night, seeing my parents fight
It was coming to my exams and I lost all my focus
My parents fighting constantly, they didn't even notice
I failed my exam and my heart full-on sank
My parents were not impressed
While I was super stressed
It came to a point I was always crying
My parents told me they were fine
But I knew they were lying
When my parents divorced
I wasn't surprised
I was at my mum's half of the week
And my dad's the other
So there were no goodbyes
I started to feel better with the help of my friends
I'm really happy now and I don't pretend.

Jasmine Le (12)
Blessed Thomas Holford Catholic College, Altrincham

Perfection

Designated calmness
Riveted through the stifling, silent air,
Breathing, sleeping, eating, surviving,
A never-ending life of conflict, the promise of tomorrow held in the balance.
Living to work, working to live,
Two imperfectly perfect lies, both guaranteed,
Who shall be chosen to win this insufferable race of life?
This, only time could tell.
An idyllic life:
Adventure, power, money, discovery,
How temporarily fulfilling.
Mountains that reach for the sky and caves that hide underneath plain soil,
Oceans of wonder and dreams,
What a disillusioned way of life.
Azure blue skies and creeping clouds
People who have the permission to breathe,
What this illusion cannot hide is
The mass of corruption and the undying darkness hiding in plain sight.
This perfect society thrives on death,
Due to an unfinished symphony of misguided violence
How undeniably cruel
A perfect pinnacle of overpowering greed and the underlying stench of desire

Lingering like perfume,
What an incredibly perfect society to survive in,
Love, money, war, this is our humanity.

Olivia Burgess (13)
Blessed Thomas Holford Catholic College, Altrincham

I Hate Warm Weather

I hate warm weather.
I hate how the sun,
Grabs onto your skin.
I hate sitting outside, sweating,
I'd rather be inside, chilling.
And I hate playing sports,
And I hate wearing shorts.
I hate everything about the warm weather.

I love the cold weather,
Although it's happening less.
I miss having a massive jumper on my chest.
I miss going outside,
And feel my hands go red.
I miss being able to sleep,
And just stay in bed.

I miss the cold weather,
The freezing cold snow,
I barely see the sheets of white,
Outside of my window,
And waking up when it's dark.
Earth is getting hotter forever.
There is so much we can do to fix that,
Together.

Maja Kieltyka (13)
Blessed Thomas Holford Catholic College, Altrincham

How Can You Say You Know?

How can you say you know
When all you have seen is my skin and not the wilderness lurking beyond the inside of me?
That swelling inside of me
You are unable to hear my bones creaking and shattering like glass
You have not swam through my veins and met everything that is going on in me
You have not been here long enough, not yet
You haven't climbed the branches on each lung to listen to how I breathe in despair
Don't mark me with your fingerprints if you plan on leaving with no other choice
If my winter is too cold, you don't deserve my spring or summer.

Harley Valentine (12)
Blessed Thomas Holford Catholic College, Altrincham

What's To Come In 2022?

2021 was a ride, pandemics and Christmas, I'm sure you'll find
From big Boris' bashes to massive laughs
And no one knew what they were up to
We hung on a thread of lockdown rules
While people could go to big public pools
The masks weren't hard but people would part with all new news
And new-founded views
In 2022, we see the end of vaccines and masks, like the east end
We find peace with new hope that we got told about from the Pope
In 2022.

Adam Murch (12)
Blessed Thomas Holford Catholic College, Altrincham

Environments Change

Our environment is failing
Time is racing
The government isn't thinking
About the problem we're facing

The world is filled
To the brim with pollution
Yet, barely anyone is
Trying to think of a solution

We need to make a change
Before it's too late
And before someone says
We'll do it at a later date.

Anna Rose McCarthy (11)
Blessed Thomas Holford Catholic College, Altrincham

Just Everything

It's not good to be good at everything,
Well, it is, just not, you know,
Everything,
I mean, you can be good at sports,
But be terrible at maths,
Or amazing at writing
But rubbish at explaining things,
I'm not saying it's bad to be good at things,
No,
But being bad at lots of things is good,
Or maybe confidence,
Yes,
People are good at being confident,
Everyone has confidence, just some don't express it,
And when you think you're not good at something,
You feel that your confidence just slips out of your head,
Now, you're not happy,
But you're still good at things,
But you still aren't happy,
Why?
Because you're not good at everything,
But, so what, who cares, really?
You'll get there eventually,
And with practice, you'll succeed,

Nearly,
But so what if you can't draw a picture perfectly,
So what if you can't learn 100 digits of pi,
So what if you can't stand up in front of a crowd and sing
your heart out,
Even so,
You're not good at everything,

Who cares if they judge you for being you?
Or what does it matter that they don't like him for being
him?
What's the problem with her being her?
It's not being good at everything that matters,
It's you,
You,
Just be you and what you're good at,
My friend,
Don't feel confident? Don't think you're good enough?
It's okay,
Because it's you,
After all,
You're not good at everything.

Siobhan S
Brayton Academy, Selby

What We Do To The Earth

The Earth,
A joyous, happy place,
All its wildlife,
Will put a smile on your face.

Except for them,
They are the monsters,
Who tear us apart,
They are the monsters,
Who break our loving hearts.

They rip up our forests,
Pollute our seas,
They warm up our planet,
And do it with ease.

All of our land,
Suddenly gone.
No more of the birds,
To sing their sweet song.

All of the horses,
Galloped away,
Yet hundreds of us die,
Every day.

As their population grows,
So do their towns.
And the more of them there are,
The less of us is to be found.

Dead as a dodo,
Is a common phrase,
Well, it was the monsters who killed them off too,
Back in the old days.

The Tasmanian tiger,
Now sadly gone.
Banished to the list,
That goes on and on.

However, those who weren't killed,
And there weren't very many,
Were shipped off to farms,
To make products like dairy.

Or taken to houses,
To eat all they wished,
Then it was off with their heads,
Swish, swish, swish.

Now, I think it's time,
We named these horrible beasts.
They are the humans,
And they respect us the very least.

So, do you hear us?
Will you now stop?
Or will you keep going,
'Til there are no more trees left to chop?

Riley Martin (11)
Brayton Academy, Selby

From Me To You

You don't hear anyone who's not the same
Yet you won't take the blame
Not everyone is like you!
Are you really that annoyed about what people do?

Put it all in the past, let everyone be free
I am different to you and you are different to me
You go around saying people aren't normal
This is very much quite uninformed.

Everyone has the right to be who they are
Not have to live up to your perceived bar
Saying that people need to change
Not showing understanding is quite strange.

People are all different, from black to white
Short, tall, all different in height
Everyone together in the same room
And all you do is judge and presume.

Not everyone is bad because they aren't like you
But if you only knew!
People don't need to change
Just to fit within your range.

Anna Davies (12)
Brayton Academy, Selby

Cracks

The shards of the mirror fall and shatter
Into a million pieces, faces twisted and morphed
People left to pick up the pieces that no longer fit together
Screens filled with perfect people, perfect lives
Then the phones crack, broken and people look with tearful eyes
Wishing they were perfect
But these lives aren't perfect
These people aren't perfect
They are moulded to be in that frame
The mould is sculpted by our society, it breaks
Happiness twists different lives
To be someone else's perfect
And the ones who can't change with a feeling of being outcast
It is time to break the mould
Shape the pieces of the mirror to fit everybody's unique and beautiful frame
Time to empower, not change.

Erin Poulton (12)
Brayton Academy, Selby

Alternate Universe

Life is twisted,
Misshapen in its utter confusion,
The world's a disaster,
With its animals, seas and trees,
People changing our visions,
Making us feel hatred towards our bodies,
Putting us through the unnecessary pain,
Just to make us feel beautiful like we belong,
This isn't the world we should be living in,
We should all be living in harmony, with no poverty or wars,
No hate, no crime and no oppression towards each other,
No animals dying, no plastic in our oceans and no trees cut
down,
People will be living with hope and feeling comfortable in
their own skin,
This is what I dream of at night,
Can we make this dream a reality?

Ella Lofthouse (12)
Brayton Academy, Selby

Standards

Fix your teeth
Brush your hair
We don't like you anyway
Change your style
Change your size
Give me a break
Once in a while
Lose some weight
Sort out your face
All this pressure
In my brain
Ugly
Disgrace
Weirdo
Shame
Get rid of the pain
It's all too much

Fix your attitude
Brush up on your manners
I don't need your opinion
Change your style
Change your mind
Give it a rest
Once in a while
Lose the standards

Sort out your expectations
All those words
Crowded my brain
Horrid
Mean
Rude
Bully
Get rid of those memories
It's all just a game.

Kayleigh Ramsay (11)
Brayton Academy, Selby

Cara

I've kept my promise
Of what I would do
To continue to live
But just without you

I get up each morning
I get through the day
Struggling past tears
Every step of the way

I go on with life
With a forced happy face
My heart aches badly
For what I can't replace

I don't know what to do
To deaden this pain
It's so hard here, without you
Where I must remain

But I will keep my promise
And I must believe
That you will be waiting
When it's my time to leave

For now, I'm being you
An independent, strong character
For what I believe
Will always come true.

Eva Dobson-Hainsworth (13)
Brayton Academy, Selby

Frightful Floods

As I sit at the window,
Staring at the storm,
I often want to know,
Why rain has become the norm.

It rises, rises and rises,
Creeping dangerously into people's lives,
But it seems like that's the way it is,
As the riverbank swells, we dive for survival.

Are we doing enough?
We talk about climate change,
We talk about it being enough,
But there's so much to rearrange.

Building flood defences,
Protecting our homes,
From steel girders to iron fences,
We are the people who feel it in our bones.

We can make the change,
We have the power.

Josh Lodge (11)
Brayton Academy, Selby

In The Shadows

In the shadows, lurking out of sight,
Are men and women with generous offers.
Love and protection, and all those other things Mum and
Dad wouldn't get you.
In the shadows, at the end of the dark alley,
You now owe your new friend.
Your mission is simple,
Just go to the next town over,
And give this guy a backpack full of,
Well, you don't know what,
In the shadows,
You find yourself trapped.
There's no way out,
Or no way out without serious consequences,
And you're now a victim of county lines,
Hidden, in the shadows.

Elizabeth Nicholson (13)
Brayton Academy, Selby

I Am The World

I am the world,
The thing you ruin every day,
Change is normal,
But not in this way,
Realise what you have done,
Help make it different,
Factories don't care,
They are the reason,
Trees help me out,
But people don't see them,
You need to stop,
Please help me out,
Change is normal,
Without a doubt.
One world is all you have,
Try making a small difference,
You might just see,
The things I have been given,
I am the world,
But soon may be gone,
If you can help,
You might not be the only one.

Ava Campbelll (11)
Brayton Academy, Selby

Global Warming

Icebergs are melting, sea levels are rising
We're not too late, but no one is helping.
Factories are working and toxins are spilling,
The ozone is crumbling and we won't stop putting chemicals
in but we're trying to breathe.
Our future is stolen and we are the thieves
Our forests are turning to ash in a second
We need to get out, we need to break free
We need to take action, it can't just be me,
That helps the world, that makes it safe
That makes this world a better place.

Isla Norris (11)
Brayton Academy, Selby

I Don't Believe In Me!

I am useless
And I will never believe that
I can do anything I set my mind to
I never doubt that
I am always worse than others
Stop saying that
I am strong inside
I tell you this
Strength means nothing
Don't ever tell me that
Caring, sharing and laughter is strength
I would say that
Confidence is worthless
I just don't admit that
A caring person is one who is there
When everyone always disappears

Now, read from the bottom up.

Lucy Minter (11)
Brayton Academy, Selby

Flower

Like a flower in a desert,
I had to grow on my own,
In the driest of weather,
Trying to stay alive.

Trying not to crumble,
Trying not to break,
But it was only a crack away,
From falling, failing or dying.

Put up a fight, expect no defeat,
Practice what you preach,
Walk and lead.
You come through what you go through,
And push through what you have to.
Keep trying.

Ciara May (13)
Brayton Academy, Selby

I Alone Am Different

I am nobody, who are you?
I am my family,
My stars,
I am my country,
Not your beating bag,
Not your litter,
I am myself,
I am not a giant,
I am not weird,
I am just different,
I am my memories,
I choose love over fear,
Not hate or judgement,
I don't judge a book by its cover,
I'm proud to be myself.
Not anyone else, just me.
Only me...

Zuzia Nejman
Brayton Academy, Selby

Empowered

E verything and all is just what you want it to be
M oments you believe that you can do it, you can
P ower the worrying times
O vercome the tiring obstacles
W onder and dream you can do anything
E verything you work for you will achieve
R ead, write, empower
E ducate yourself
D on't give up on your dreams.

Seth Wratten (11)

Brayton Academy, Selby

How The Animals Survive

The animals on Earth are telling a story
Of how they fear us not being sorry
Chopping down trees
Polluting the seas
Turtles and fish drowning in plastic
Polar bears' ice and caps melting is drastic
Why can't we just see that if this carries on
Then in two or five years, they will all be gone!

Lorelai Drury (11)
Brayton Academy, Selby

We Are All The Same

We are all born equal, that's what they say
But what if you're different
And go your own way
You may face prejudice
Hatred
It's bad
That the world we live in
Can make you so sad
So rise up
Be strong
Never be ashamed
We are all just the same.

Elliot Smith (11)
Brayton Academy, Selby

Forever Friends

Friends are like family,
When I'm alone, they are there,
And when I'm sad,
They always care.

What a joy it is,
To have friends that I love,
The nature of friendship,
Is... people who I will always trust.

Phoebe Hepworth (12)
Brayton Academy, Selby

My Future Self

Dear future self, may I ask you something, please?
How is Harry Potter Studios, how is your life?
Is there a new top game, do you have a wife?
Do my eyes get better, do I graduate?
The answers, I cannot wait.

Dear future self, may I ask you something, please?
How was high school, did you get new friends?
The questions won't stop, they won't end.
Did you get a dog, have pandas gone extinct?
Have you found what's lost, does my brother still stink?

Dear future self, may I ask you something, please?
Did Boris resign, do I score for my football team?
Could you tell me if I achieve my dream?
I have many enquiries to ask today,
Are there still rhinos in the world, do I have good pay?

Dear future self, may I ask you something, please?
Do you have a good home and family?
Have you got children, are you living happily?
How do you feel, can you draw with ease?
One last question, will you write back, please?

Max Dickinson (12)
Campsmount Academy, Norton

Why?

Stop
Don't hurt me
Just leave me be
Out of this prison cell
Set me free

My life is a trap
Full of pain
Every day is torture
You beat me with a cane

Why call me names?
I just become sad
I've lost my identity
All it does is makes me mad

All the things you have done
Come back to me every day
It's like a wave of fear
In every single way

My life should be good
Except you make it bad
How can you be so cruel?
I'm just a little lad

All you do is abuse me
In every single way
Mentally and physically
Why does your anger stay?

Your words can hurt
As bad as a punch
Why do you do it?
To show off to your bunch

You may be cruel
You may be mean
But believe me
I'll make myself seen.

Matilda Porter (11)
Campsmount Academy, Norton

Creativity Is What?

Creativity is what makes us unique
Like the people who have climbed to Everest's peak
Without creativity, the world would be bleak
The world was silent until someone figured out how to speak

If no one thought outside of the box
Your imagination would have a lock
Breaking the mould, don't put it to a stop
Using your mind, you can turn into The Rock
Or dive sixty feet, or drive a ship from the dock

In a daydream, you can let your brain run wild
Or rewind time to when you were a child
Or cancel the Amazon Prime that you trialled
That'll never happen, even I'm in denial

With a little bit of brainpower, you can achieve big things
So be creative and spread your wings
Don't act like a puppet on strings
Leap higher than you could even think.

Charlie Brooks (11)
Campsmount Academy, Norton

Dear Future Me

Hello, it's your old self here,
Do you remember me?
If so, remember all those fun times,
I know I don't get to see you, but you get to see me,
Through memories,
How has our family and your life been?
What has happened through the years?
I know I will never know,
The past will never know about the future, but the future will
know about the past,
If they remember it,
Are you married or single?
Do you have children like you wanted?
Are you rich or are you not?
How old are you, what year is it?
What historic events have happened throughout the years?
Will you write another poem in the future?
Hopefully, you're having the best life ever,
Good luck in your future, Maisie.

Maisie Hatfield (11)
Campsmount Academy, Norton

Life Is Strange

Although someone may seem happy
Always remember looks can be deceiving
Don't bully others, karma exists
Just remember, you can resist

No matter what happens
Remember to try
If it fails more, just don't cry
Unless you want your mummy
To bake you an apple pie
It's not the end of the world
You won't die

In bad, there is always good
If therapy doesn't help, nor will food
Don't be depressed, don't be emo
If you do, it won't boost your ego
All it will do is make you cruel
Don't hide in the dark
Because then, your dog will bark
Just remember, be yourself.

Niko Cala
Campsmount Academy, Norton

Future Me

Dear future me,
Life is currently like being stuck in a tree.
I hope life is good for you,
I hope our dreams all come true.

Dear future me,
Our lives have been strange, do you agree?
Has our brother yet moved out?
And Dad's still bragging, without a doubt.

Dear future me
The hill is not that steep
But after all, you won't stop
And you haven't let the balloon go pop.

You're a bowling ball
Life?
You make them fall
And don't forget to take out the bins.

Ben Chambers (12)
Campsmount Academy, Norton

Empowered

Don't let anyone tear you down
Believe in yourself, no matter what
You can do anything if you believe
If people tear you down, get straight back up

Don't let anyone tell you that you won't succeed
Always do good deeds
Help anyone believe in themselves

Tell everyone to believe and never lose hope
Always help anyone in need
Don't give up, hoping it's the only way you'll cope
Never give up or you may lose
Help anyone to stop all the abuse.

Rihanna Brooke Simmons (12)
Campsmount Academy, Norton

Save The Sea

Plastic in the sea
Nobody will help, except for me
Go outside and you will see

Plastic on the beach, spilling into the sea
Fish are dying, don't you agree?
Go outside and you will see

Please don't dump into the sea
It kills the fish and the sea
Go outside and you will see

Now, come and help me.

Rhys Bailey (11)
Campsmount Academy, Norton

Shine Bright

Keep positive
You shine so bright
You never go out like a light
So what if you're strange?
So what if you have fame?
You should never change
You shine your light so others can see
Just sail in the sea
But remember
No others can be like me.

Brooklyn Johnson (11)
Campsmount Academy, Norton

The Everlasting Cave

Love, an everflowing lake
No matter what, that lake will never dry out
This is what I call unconditional love
This love cannot be forced as it might have a lake
But that lake will be an everlasting lake
As it will be a never flowing lake
That's the difference between the two types of love in my opinion
And how I view them
Happiness, a cave filled with green in every corner
The sound of the waves from the blue lake
The lingering feeling of the air on the skin
This is what I call self-love
The sounds of the waves
Those inner thoughts of mine
Those lingering feelings that inner peace which one longs for
The greenish places are my values
The flourishing blue lake is my desire filled with desires
Those desires
The cave itself is me, myself and I
In the true nature of my true self
Leading to self-awareness, self-love, self-improvement
Self-discipline and self-respect
The everlasting cave.

Haddijatou Sarr (18)

Fortis Academy, Great Barr

Empowered

Today it's clear of the rose-tinted foundations holding up
society,
And when you look closer, you can't help but worry for
humanity,
But the glass will shatter and the facade will fade,
It is difficult for us to consider what a mess we've made,
From our actions, I'm wondering how we will end up,
When our youth is out here carrying weapons, please don't
just stop,
Why do we care so much when our body and our face
Don't match the filtered snaps?
Your beauty shouldn't go to waste,
But it's not easy under constant pressure, they judge as they
scroll,
To all my brothers and sisters, underneath, you're pretty
rock and roll,
Then when we begin to agree and see discrimination unfold,
And then we soon realise that history is not in fact history at
all,
And although the form of slavery in 1850 is no longer,
It's easy for people to forget how far we've come,
Our unity is a bit stronger,
But it still hurts when it's people of a minority race,
Still cannot gain the same opportunities, working harder for
that place,

But, let me send a message to all of you out there,
Society is painted in pink and it's just not fair,
Deception and hypocrisy stitched into the hierarchy,
And it's no joke so please take this seriously,
To the victims of society in any shape or form,
Now, it's time for us to rise above and help us all,
Thank you for reading if you made it this far,
But your job doesn't end here, it's only just begun,
Take the time, to reiterate the injustice of this world,
And touch the heart of even one, to grant us what we
deserve.

Mimha Choudhury (17)
Fortis Academy, Great Barr

To Me

The difference is seen as negativity,
If that girl or that boy doesn't look right in society's eyes,
They're an automatic outcast,
When you see Winnie Harlow, what do you think?
I bet it's her different skin,
Her vitiligo clouds your opinion,
When in reality, she should be seen as a beautiful black girl,
Who attracts attention everywhere she goes,
Because she is different,
Who sets the standards on what we should be?
Who sets the standards on what we should look like or who
we should be?
Are we not all born different, naturally?
There's so much more to your makeup than make-up,
There's so much more to your style than fashion,
What really should matter to others is your drive and your
passion,
Michael Jackson changed his appearance, what for?
When his music spoke for itself.
The pressures and views of others on what you need to be
accepted in, society, have people looking not only the same
but crazy,
Can't you see?
Everybody should be different,
Because actually, underneath the physicality,

Of what we all seem to see, is just surface,
Scratched away to reveal underneath that,
We are all different!

Senai Thompson (15)
Fortis Academy, Great Barr

Dear Women

To the women who are discriminated against,
Who don't show they're vulnerable,
I'm sorry you're so hated,
The world needs to be humbled,
You're loved, you're admired,
I'm sorry you're holding the pain,
People need to know this isn't just a game,
It's not a joke, they can't solve the problem within,
It's not a joke, they can't see past,
The colour of someone's skin,
Whether they're laughing at her hijab,
Or her white friend earning more,
Women of ethnic minorities,
You are worth fighting for!

To the women who are working,
To every mom,
Trying to put food on the table for,
Their little girl or son,
Working so hard, in a job you don't like,
Doing the worrying and discipline,
To the housework,
To the work shifts at night,
You're doing a great job.
It's admirable how you're still smiling,
You're inspiring, you're commendable.

No, you're not failing
So, hold yourself with dignity,
It's what you deserve,
You are and always will be the best mum in the whole world.

Nuha Choudhury (17)
Fortis Academy, Great Barr

Lockdown

24th March, 2020, we locked down
Our whole country simply shut down
Everyone adapting to working from home
Charging like bulls into the unknown
Not knowing how long
We'd be repeating the same song
Stay home, control the virus, save lives
So we stayed home, like bees in hives

On the 31st of October, a second lockdown
Everyone felt a little down
To hear such bad news on Halloween
Oh Boris, how mean
Everyone went back to daily walks
And tuning in to the government talks
Hoping to again be free
A vaccine could be key

On the 6th of January, guess what, a third lockdown
Still can't travel to the town
Can't see family and friends
Beginning to think this won't end
But everyone kept on going
Dissatisfaction growing
But foreseen
We finally had a vaccine

Fingers crossed, we are now not in lockdown
Everyone is beginning to frown
At our prime minister
Doing something sinister
Breaking his own lockdown rules
Making him look like a fool
But we are just grateful
That the lockdown in our country
Is no longer shut down.

Samuel Adamson-Clarke (16)
Fortis Academy, Great Barr

'Twixt Th'moon 'Nd Th'worm

'Twixt the moon and sea th'worm wiggled,
little it was and through its celluloid mind
small strings of thoughts configured,
moulding and folding into the rocky mountain
the stars seemed to fade away into those dreary clouds
dropping down to the now misty floor of pebbles and stones
crumbling underneath the worm's body
and through the mist shone hazes of hues visible in
th'worm's tiny tunnel vision:
pea-green for the world it lived in, cobalt for the sky
above, golden for the longing of th'sun and
cherry red for its little
heart beating to keep it alive
th'little worm wiggled, its thought-strings
shaped into images of the other side
plants sprouting in shades of pistachio and moss
and the electric blue of life waiting to meet it,
aching in the reds of the love-
onward the worm wiggled (following
its brain thoughts in silhouettes of squiggle)
to the top of the rocky mountain.

Jani Birdi (17)
Fortis Academy, Great Barr

Faith

Terrorism, shooting, wars, words, narrow-minded
Associated with Islam
But if only they knew
Peace, love, compassion
Are the true meanings of Islam

Let the driver drive, don't be fooled by illusions of this world
Remember, if it costs your peace
It's too expensive
Slow down in life
Before you become the victim of your own desires
Work hard, don't give up
Because many people think life is like a booking
And you could reserve your place
Planting the seeds of Hell
Yet expecting the bliss of Heaven
So much killing and terror
We have become immune to violence.
Take care of your faith before it's too late.

Aissa Seckan (16)
Fortis Academy, Great Barr

La Verita (The Truth)

Everybody wonders what life is about
What success looks like
Is it about money, about fame
Or just a public perception of people's desires?
No, it's about living, about learning from previous mistakes
About progressing
Which could be seen as socially and mentally
Not just financially
Our society puts too much emphasis on what it was
Rather than what it could be, with self-determination
Self-belief is not about being overconfident
But it's about accepting your faults
And finding a way to progress
Trust the process.

Hartson Isibor (17)
Fortis Academy, Great Barr

Mine And Yours

Lies, lies, and more lies,
My life is built off of lies,
Your life is built off of lies,
We look to our phones for beauty,
But that beauty lies in your eyes
Not your face, not your body, but your kind
Stop looking to that model or celebrity online
And look at that person I see before my eyes
So pretty, so bright, your whole face shines
Why don't you see what I see through my eyes?
You are not a canvas
Nor are you an edit that can be fabricated in real life
Your body, your face, your mind is beautiful, and so is mine.

Tenayha Buchanan (16)

Fortis Academy, Great Barr

In My Skin

Wherever they go,
They get looks and stares,
But little do they know,
We don't really care.
Some have had it since birth,
Some have had it since eleven,
The patch carries a worth,
A clever gift from Heaven.
We wear it with pride,
It is truly embraced.
It is carried in our stride.
We don't feel displaced.
We won't be concerned,
And it won't be upsetting.
It is key we all learn,
Vitiligo is a blessing.

Amaani Azad (17)
Fortis Academy, Great Barr

I Am A Black Woman

I am a black woman
I am not appreciated by our men
I am full of love but only receive lust
I am not needed
Nor am I wanted
But I gave birth to you all
You should appreciate me
You should love me
Without me, there wouldn't be you
I love my features, my hair and beauty
You dehumanise and mock me
I am powerful, I know my worth
My existence is a blessing, not a curse
You will not break me
I am a black woman.

Lesharn Francis (16)
Fortis Academy, Great Barr

Emptiness

Emptiness is what I'm in possession of,
It is what my head is filled with,
What I need is love,
Even though I know that it's an enormous myth.

Happiness is what I love and need,
At some point to get it, you'll need to pay a fee.
I'm chasing my dreams and I follow my greed,
Happiness is what I love and need.

Maksymilian Grzegorzewski (16)
Fortis Academy, Great Barr

Words On A Page

A haiku

The words on the page
Are speaking my inner thoughts
I feel empowered.

Ellena Stanley (16)

Fortis Academy, Great Barr

Boris The Rule Breaker

B ring your own bottle to Number 10
O ld people left to suffer alone
J acked up on gin and juice
O ld people left to suffer alone

P rime minister broke the rules
M ocked the Queen at her husband's funeral.

Ben Dickinson (14)
Kirk Hallam Support Centre, Kirk Hallam

Prime Minister Is A Joker

B eing a bad influence on people.

O ld people left to die.

J uice and gin flowing freely.

O ld people left to die.

P artying all night at Number 10

M ocking the Queen, no dignity seen.

Pip O'Dwyer (14)
Kirk Hallam Support Centre, Kirk Hallam

The Threat Of Russia

R ussia threaten to invade
U kraine the target of their raid
S oldiers waiting
S everal thousand deaths are pending
I nternational politics in crisis
A resolution can be found.

Ryan Hinman (14)
Kirk Hallam Support Centre, Kirk Hallam

Covid

C hildren couldn't play with their friends
O ld people die alone
V accines were made, hoorah
I n the end, the vaccine didn't work
D eath!

Lucas Walek (12)
Kirk Hallam Support Centre, Kirk Hallam

We Are Women

We rise from adversity
But we let our scars remind us
Of the prejudice, judgement and bigotry
That echoes through the halls of history

Even when our legs get tied down
With the shackles and chains of society's stereotypes
We push each other forward
Helping each powerful woman walk
We may have only moved an inch
But, to the young girls of future generations
It'll be like we stepped past the moon and stars

We will never be afraid to stand up for what is right
Equal pay, equal opportunities and equal lives

Malala never stopped when her hijab was drowning in blood
And, Burnita Shelton Matthews
Who helped pave the way for girls to thrive in a male-
dominated environment
Never halted at a brick wall

We have been screaming for decades
Yet, no one has heard our cries
It's just a gentle murmur in the background
Ignored

Women we designed to be admired
People say
These words get etched into the clay-like minds of children

But, we implore you to realise
That women are fierce, determined and unstoppable
We should never be held back by others' forceful grip
Or be on a pedestal as a Russian doll
Empty
Only to be noticed by fleeting eyes
As we are all equals in this imperfect world.

Daisy Cook (16)
Lymm High School, Lymm

Why?

Who am I? Who is she? Who is he?
I'm different to her, he is different to me.
I hate arrogance but do the arrogant hate themselves?
I'm okay with capitalism,
But, are the capitalists?
I like shopping, but do the workers?
I love animals, but do they love us?

Humans, hateful, useless, malicious, arrogant, narcissistic, superstitious,
But, are we? Who decided this? Whose opinion? Why do some believe this?
Why do some not? Why?

I think Ross and Rachel were on a break, but why do I?
I think equality is important, but why do I?
I think that the world is worth saving, but why do I?
I think Capri Suns are amazing, but why do I?
I think the education system is a joke, but why do I?
I think I'm lucky, but why do I?
Why do I think this?
Is it because I'm different to her?
Or because he is different to me?
Are my differences a weakness, or do they empower me?

Harriet Dougall (14)
Lymm High School, Lymm

Endless

To no end does the wind weave through the trees,
and make the sorrowful grass ripple like the gentle waves of tropical seas.
To no end does the sun rise and fall over the ever-distant horizon,
many years of wisdom in its fiery eye.
To no end does everything begin, end and begin anew,
the life thriving and fading, growing and being lost.

Oceans and valleys the world has been,
deserts and mountains, forests and jungles.
Many a star the world has seen, fiery, bright, streaking across the sky.
Many a day, a year or more, the world has spent,
pondering its endless knowledge under sun and moon.

Until the end does the wind weave and fly, the sun rises and falls over the sky.
Until the end, there is the life that grows and thrives and ends and ends.
But, all the world will wait for one true end and that end will take it all.

Noah Richardson (11)
Lymm High School, Lymm

I Look Out The Window

I look out the window,
There are polluting machines,
Surrounded by dead trees,

I look out the window,
There are butterflies, flying by,
Destined to live a ten-day life,
Before they cripple and die,

I look out the window,
The next generation,
Supposed saviours of the world,
Littering and kicking trees,

I look out the window,
Buildings and roads penetrating the land,
Standing on the land where meadows used to be abundant,
Where animals could run free,

I look out the window,
To see,
Death,
Destruction,
Cruelty to nature.

Scarlett Gould (12)
Lymm High School, Lymm

Cyber-Bullying

If you're on websites, apps or games,
You will be called lots of names,
Most of these people try and strive,
But then the words will eat them alive,

Just one click and it's gone for good,
But everyone else will give you a push,
People will judge you and make you fall,
But your power will try to make you stand up tall,

Heart throbbing and brain shattering,
You will have a fear of finally answering,
Stop saying these words and giving me fear,
Oh shut up now, and I'm telling you here!

Pia Mittag (13)
Lymm High School, Lymm

Alone

Alone,
Swathed in sweltering black,
Marinating in my own thoughts,
As I drag my pencil across,
The nostalgic feel of a tattered notebook,
And the innovative drawings of a mad woman,
Staring back,
With disapproving judgement,
Of one's own reception of reality,
Leaving you too stunned to move or breathe,
More vibrant than any planet's own patterns.

A dusty cover,
Trying, crying out to help me,
Innocence and colour.

Alanna Baker (13)
Lymm High School, Lymm

Fight Like A Girl

Girls are considered fragile
too easy to break
constantly emotional
very quick to cry
and always need help
like a damsel in distress
we are treated like dolls
shaped in the way society wants us to be
we are used as insults
you fight like a girl
men don't cry
man up
but, we are warriors
spies in disguise
cunning masterminds
we are wild
we are free
we are diamonds,
ready to be seen.

Aliyah Bakhressa (13)
Nottingham Girls' Academy, Aspley

Think

When I am alone, not playing on my phone,
I think about tomorrow, today.

I wonder if the suffering in the world will ever end.
WIll the victim and bully ever become friends?
Will the voiceless and oppressed ever liberate?
Will those desperately saving starving lives make it, or just
be too late?

I do think a lot when I'm on my own, not playing on my
phone.
I think about tomorrow, today.

I think about global peace, the middle east and all those
wasted lives,
Why don't we do enough for the vulnerable, when in nature,
only the fittest survive.
I think about mental health or the unhealthiness of the
mind,
I think about the givers, the takers, the cunning ones that
come across as kind.

I think a lot when on my own, not playing on my phone,
I think about the coming tomorrow, today.

I think somehow, just maybe, I must have gotten this wrong.
Leaders aren't born or developed, but just keep rising from
amongst the already strong,
I'm not going to ever become the real me, but just become
programmed to be another living deed.

Do you ever think when not playing on your phone?
When away from the comforts of being at home?

I think a lot when I'm on my own, not playing on my phone.

Zeeneth Araf (14)
Nottingham Girls' Academy, Aspley

Our Tragic Environment

As icebergs melt, up and down below.
Animals are quickly scavenging for a new home.
Endangered creatures dying one by one,
Will climate change ever end?

Vehicles zooming past us every day
But do they know what people have to face?
Factories carelessly polluting the Earth,
Is there really a Planet B?

Violent waves getting hungrier each second,
Corpses of fish lying unconsciously.
Heat strengthening every minute,
Is there a solution to this mystery?

Plastic and glass piling higher and higher,
It's a never-ending "mistake".
The environment around us gets filled with litter,
But without a trace.

A voice must be heard,
Before this affects those across the planet,
In order to save the environment,
Let's help protect our world!

Julia Borucinska (11)
The Aylesbury Vale Academy, Aylesbury

Running To A Dream

If I could run away, find a place to stay
I'd dive into a dream
One where I could scream
At last, a place filled with joy
Nothing to avoid

Running away in a dream is up to how far you go, if you
don't try then you'll never know
All the sorrow and darkness will then be far gone
You could lay there and dream all night until dawn
From then on, there will be no pain
For it would all be lost, drown in a drain
No more battles and wars or prejudice
Just one big utopia that will never fall
The fantasies we learn all through our lives
They are my escapes, the things that I thrive.

Chloe Evans (11)
The Aylesbury Vale Academy, Aylesbury

Pretty On The Inside

All these gorgeous girls and handsome boys
They fit so well
But there is a secret that I would like to tell
Not even one person is perfect
It's true, but one person that's really pretty is you
So don't worry, be happy
Look in the mirror and admire yourself
You only live once, so go ahead
You're amazing, you're pretty, smile
Don't you think that?
Make sure to love the skin you're in
Love the beautiful spots on your face
Love your attractive eyes
And trust me
You will have your best life!

Ellina Sarpong (12)
The Aylesbury Vale Academy, Aylesbury

She Made Me See

I look at myself and see skin and bones
Sometimes, I wonder if I'm without soul
Or if I'm a clone
There's nothing I enjoy, no emotions within
Maybe that's a recent change or maybe that's how it's always been
But recently, I've seen her, all pale and fair
And there she stands, radiating positive air
I love how it is when she's around
She is sweet and soft
And my love for her is oh, so profound
One look at her and I feel at peace
I truly feel she is my one release from this false-hearted world.

Alexandra Jordaan (12)
The Aylesbury Vale Academy, Aylesbury

Empowerment

How do we truly empower other people?
By having the strength to make all things equal?
To fight for what's right, or make a stand?
Against inequality of woman or man?

Many people throughout our past,
Have marched and protected until new laws were passed.
The Bryant and May Matchgirl strikes,
Saw industrial action for human rights.
Workers stood against long working days,
And serious health issues and poor pay,
These strikes led to a better work life,
Empowering children, husband and wife.

For centuries, women have been on crusades,
For more representation or equal pay,
All thanks to Pankhurst and her suffragettes,
Women got the vote to say what's next.

When Rosa Parks got on the bus,
Refusing to give up her seat caused a fuss,
But she stood against racial segregation,
Black people were empowered because of her
demonstration.

Today, there are laws against human violation,
Empowering LGBT communities through education,

Many have fought for equal opportunities,
To dispel discrimination and create unity.

Empowerment can be given to so many situations,
Social, economical, political and education,
We must find all the strength to help others find,
A place of equality, where people are kind.

Make others confident,
Don't crush their dreams,
Or control others' lives,
Help them, by all means.

Millie Trafford (12)
The FitzWimarc School, Rayleigh

The Rainbow

The rainbow of empowerment, the aftermath of darkness,
A helping hand in stormy times, telling you to carry on.

Red is for resilience, carrying on all the time,
Staying strong, enduring.
Orange is optimism, smiling,
Laughing, making people happy,
Yellow is for yippee, celebrating achievement,
A light goes against the dark, pushing back the sadness,
Growth is green, learning from mistakes,
Nurturing from failure, stronger every day,
Blue stands for bravery, courageous and strong,
A rock, a helpful shelter of bravery,
Indigo is inspiring and violet is a vivid imagination,
Both go hand in hand, beautiful and colourful.
That is the rainbow, keep looking for it.

Grace King (11)
The FitzWimarc School, Rayleigh

Rise

I come from a home of blood and dirt.
I've taught myself to block out the hurt.
I never knew the true meaning of love.
I found myself praying to the sky above.

But, as the seasons flipped and changed.
I learned that love must be exchanged.
For, I must let the world have my heart,
In hopes of receiving my special part.

In order for us to rise once more.
We have to end this mighty war.
People will come and go as they please,
But never bow upon your knees.

Be proud of who you are today.
Because you are worth it in every way.
So, next time, you feel like you're not enough.
Be brave and show them that you are tough.

Mia Warwick (14)
The FitzWimarc School, Rayleigh

Empowered

Empowerment means living beyond feelings
Beyond circumstance
Beyond what the world says you must be

Empowerment means reaching deep inside your spirits
Beyond your surface
Beyond heartache, regret and retreat

Empowerment
That is what empowerment means
For ourselves and others

It is what comes from true love
Deep within the heart

Paying it forward
To give us life
That is true empowerment

From places of true gratitude and true strength
Given as gifts from above

It is what takes you beyond the place of yesterday
And toward the place of tomorrow.

Shannon Newby (11)
The FitzWimarc School, Rayleigh

I Am...

Metal is strong, but I am stronger,
Leather is tough, but my skin is tougher.

Glass can be smashed, but I can't be broken,
Rock bottom is hard, but I'll never hit it,

Engines need power but I already have it,
Water is deep but I will always get to the surface.

You can't hurt me with a sword,
You can't hurt me with your words.

I am strong and I am unbreakable,
I am powerful and I will always find a way.

Metal is strong, but I am stronger.

Freya Bourdon (13)
The FitzWimarc School, Rayleigh

Empowerment

E very fear felt had become a reality
M emories of the past
P rospects of not succeeding
O ld wounds needing healing
W alking along, nothing mattered
E very step, getting stronger and stronger
R ealising that thoughts were now embracing
M oments, mountains climbed
E ndorsement
N ot because you cannot succeed, but
T o show that the mind is stronger than can ever be explained.

Olivia Wilkinson (11)
The FitzWimarc School, Rayleigh

My Family And I

Sun is shining,
Super bright,
Amazing days,
Enchanted nights,
Love and hope,
Is all I need,
To live days,
And nights in peace.

Home is where the heart is,
That's what they all say,
But anywhere with family,
Is still a home for me.

Through thick and thin,
They have my back,
They're my family,
I love them,
They make me strong,
They empower me,
My family and I.

Sophie Attard (11)
The FitzWimarc School, Rayleigh

Empowerment

The people these days are just like sheep
They copy each other and don't have goals
They're losing themselves
Protect your soul

I am a leader in the streets
Respect my grind
I see beauty in others
I'm a passionate guy

Be yourself and see what happens
Be classy and successful
Be patient
Respect the process

Nothing is impossible
Remember that.

Finn Tyrell (13)
The FitzWimarc School, Rayleigh

Family Love

I am brave,
I am strong,
When I'm down,
My family push me along,
When the roads seem uphill,
And instead of smiling, you sigh,
Your family will help you,
They will help you out of love,
They will be there when you cry,
My family empower me to do my best,
And that is why I'm strong and I'm brave,
Because I have them and I know that their love won't fade.

Autumn Barteluk (11)
The FitzWimarc School, Rayleigh

Stand Tall

If you get knocked down, do you need to fight?
If you get hurt, will you be alright?
If you snitch, will you be ditched?
Don't embrace the fight,
You will be alright.
Ignore them all and stand tall.

Rebecca Wilson (11)
The FitzWimarc School, Rayleigh

The Trees And Us

All trees start off as a seed in the ground
As they grow, over time, the tree will get bigger and
stronger with enough food and water
Others are not as lucky either, they grow in a place, too
sunny or too damp
A tree could live for thousands of years
Or just for a day
It's hard to say
The tree might be deformed or carved or thin, even with
some love from within
From any angle or way you look at life be happy with who
you are and be nice to others
Unless they bully you then go tell a teacher, or two.

Idris Yunus (15)
The Link Secondary School, Beddington

The Madhouse

Welcome to the madhouse,
Try to keep your sanity as you question reality.
Welcome to the madhouse,
So many voices, too many choices.
Welcome to the madhouse,
Where the lust for trust will cause you vanity.
Welcome to the madhouse,
Where reality will make you question your sanity.
All the voices, so many choices, try not to trust your sanity
while you question reality, such vanity.
Welcome to my mind.

Niall McKelvey (17)
The Link Secondary School, Beddington

The Chinese New Year Poem

In the early weeks of the year, fireworks bang in the night.
People roam in the night, holding a dragon that is taking flight.
In the night, a cleaning shall happen to keep out ghouls in the first light.
Take a picture of the perfect family, so estranged families reunite.
Have a happy new year, the streets will be bright.

Alex Francis (13)
The Link Secondary School, Beddington

What Is Love?

Love is peaceful, love is life,
Love is sometimes like a knife,
Love is sweet, love is dreams,
Is love always what it seems?
Love is strong, love is bright,
Love will always be the light.

Aiden Mottram (15)
The Link Secondary School, Beddington

One Earth

Global warming is a warning that the world is in danger,
Carry on destroying it and we'll all become strangers.
Global warming is a warning that this world is a mess,
Carry on destroying it, could we care any less?

This Earth was amazing, with different combinations,
But in the 21st century, we have ruined God's creation.
This Earth was amazing, with wonders aplenty,
But in the 21st century, it is the past that we envy.

From the top of the mountains to the depths of the sea,
This Earth is high in minerals but low in generosity.
From the top of the mountains to the depths of the sea,
This Earth is plentiful and is here for you and me.

We're seven billion people on the world's stage,
On the verge of a new story, chapter, page.
We're seven billion people, whose habits must re-arrange,
One Earth, one chance, it's time for a change.

Ksanette Samrai (11)
The Sacred Heart Language College, Wealdstone

The Things That Make My Heart Warm

The things that make my heart warm,
Jumping on the trampoline whilst my dad mows the lawn,
Telling ghost stories in an evening storm,
A mug of hot chocolate before jumping into bed,
My cat purring against my tired, little head,
The things that make my heart warm,
Relaxing in a lovely, hot bubble bath,
My dad tickling my feet whilst I loudly laugh,
Skating down my road, the wind brushing against my face,
My neighbour came out with a big smile, holding his briefcase.
The things that make my heart warm,
Tightly hugging my sister, as if I haven't seen her in a year,
Winning a netball match with my team as we joyfully cheer,
Going on walks just before night-time,
Picking up a good book, wanting to read it for a lifetime.
The things that make my heart warm,
Watching the sunset on top of a steep hill,
My dad's face when he sees the restaurant bill,
Excitedly rushing to my favourite lesson,
My mum cooking my favourite dinner, mmm, I feel like I'm in heaven.
The things that make my heart warm,
Watching a movie with popcorn and sweets,

My mum home, with McDonald's to eat,
Seeing my best friend in what has felt like forever,
I will never let go of you, never ever!

Coleen Moran (12)
The Sacred Heart Language College, Wealdstone

My City

My city has a lot of faces,
Perhaps a few hidden in blood-curdling places,
Flung open is your emotional gate,
When you realise you're headed for a gruesome fate.

And yet I dream of a better city and world,
Where everywhere you go, there aren't knives being hurled,
And where love isn't just observed, but returned and
confirmed,
And where over drugs and alcohol, family is preferred.

So, stand up together, united as a people.
Please,
Help the bees,
Plant more trees,
Clean the seas.

And when you're beaten down for you are in this life,
Try again.
Donate to charity,
Connect with others and yet be full of rarity.
You don't have to be a celebrity,
To inspire people and be full of clarity.

So yes,
Maybe sometimes we feel like we're just one of millions,
trillions, billions of fish in the ocean,
But maybe, we're all just putting in a minuscule portion, all
stirred up to create a potion,

Of our devotion,
For the next generation.

You have a voice, whether you're five or 105,
Every,
Single,
One of us does,
Never forget that.

Kitty Norrington (12)
The Sacred Heart Language College, Wealdstone

Lillies Soaked In Gasoline

My skin is scarred,
My hands are raw and red,
My eyes are hollow and bare,
My hair,
My once beautiful, beautiful hair,
Has been eaten away and left,
Raw.

I am no longer beautiful,
Now, I am only scarred,
My burdens lie here in my chest,
My heart beats but I do not feel it.
I am a mess.

I used to be beautiful,
Now I am a mess.
So, I bury myself in my sorrows and hide,
I want to coat all my problems with gasoline,
Then flick a match and set fire.

I want to feel my heartbeat from underneath my chest,
I want to feel alive.
I want to feel the sights and sounds of the world,
Like a lily in a meadow, I long to thrive.

And so thrive I will,
I will grow and blossom,
Not in beauty,
Not in vain,

I do not want to be perfect anymore,
I am more than my looks,
I live to thrive,
I thrive to live,
All of love,
Not looks,
I do not live off of gasoline anymore.
Now, I live the life of the rain.

Now, I open my heart to happiness,
And burn away the agony, the guilt,
The pain.

Elishka Dodoo (14)
The Sacred Heart Language College, Wealdstone

My Perfect Parents

You gave me power when I was weak,
And always told me that I was unique,
You gave me hope when I was down,
And make me smile instead of frown.

You listened to my problems of any length,
And always gave me formidable strength.
Not only did you have great advice,
But you also encouraged me to think twice.

All the times that you were there,
Proves to me that you really care.
Right from the very start,
I've loved you with all my heart.

How did you have the energy, Mum and Dad?
To do everything that you did,
To be teachers, doctors and parents,
When I was just a little kid!

Thank you, Mum and Dad, for all the things you do,
I am extremely lucky to have loving parents like you.
For everything we shared,
The dreams, the laughter and the tears,
I love you very much,
And forever through the years.

Mehwish Herwitker (11)
The Sacred Heart Language College, Wealdstone

My City

My city has lots of places,
You'd not be wrong to call it famous,
I know that people will want to show you around,
They'll take you to see the nice parts of town,
You'll go visit the London Eye,
Or go and see Big Ben and even more,
They'll take you for a ride, it'll be exhilarating,
But, if you stick with me, I'll show you what London's really like inside,
Inequality, poverty, a society in which the rich have everything,
Just next door, there could be someone in desperate need of help,
Many don't want to acknowledge this, but if we want a change, we've got to do something,
So, come along with me and we'll find a way to do this,
Somehow, somewhere, so that everyone gets the same opportunities,
So, come join me in the fight for equality.

Maria Ottaviani (12)
The Sacred Heart Language College, Wealdstone

If I Were...

If I were a bird, I would soar high in the sky,
Watching the world below me pass by.
I would perch high up on the tallest tree,
And enjoy Mother Nature and being free.

If I were a tree, I would stand mighty and tall,
And give shelter and shade to one and all.
I would watch the children that sit around me,
And listen to their laughter with delight and glee.

If I were the sea, I would stare at the sky so bright,
And all the twinkling, sparkling stars at night.
I would lovingly reach out to the sandy shore,
And carry with me, sweet treasures and more.

If I were a flower, I would sashay and sway,
To the gentle breeze that came my way.
I would spread my fragrance to the ends of the Earth,
To trigger one's senses, for what it's worth.

Francene De Sa Pinto (11)
The Sacred Heart Language College, Wealdstone

Be You!

Sometimes, you can be very shy
Sometimes, you just want to cry
You want the ground to swallow you up
Instead, it doesn't work and you just want to give up

You know you are loved to be who you are
So please, don't be ashamed for who you are
All you want is to feel free, honestly
So, just let yourself be

All your worries can be weighing you down
So, don't make your smile into a permanent frown
Don't take a fright
This is your fight

Be you
Think it through
Don't be ashamed for what you believe
If you stand up for yourself, there will be a big relief

So, spread your wide wings
Hear the bells of wisdom ring
if anyone comes and judges you
Don't let it come to you and think it through.

Olivie Dodoo (11)
The Sacred Heart Language College, Wealdstone

Happiness Is Everywhere

Even in the moments when you don't know what to do,
Happiness is always everywhere around you,
Whenever the world turns upside down,
You don't need to show a frown,
So think of even the smallest things,
Which you think happiness brings,

Even now, with Covid 19,
Your smile should still be seen,
You got to spend more time with your family,
And you all worked independently,
So think of even the smallest things,
Which you think happiness brings,

I hope I opened your imagination,
So that you'll be happy all around the nation,
And remember that you don't always have to expect lots,
Simply just untie all of those sad knots,
So, think of even the smallest things,
Which you think happiness brings.

Nelly Materka (11)
The Sacred Heart Language College, Wealdstone

Imperfect

You're not good enough,
You can't plaster on a smile and expect it to be okay,
You could never compete,
Look at them, then look at you,
You're stranded from society,
Falling into an endless abyss,
Thoughts flood your mind,
Why can't you be perfect?
Why can't you be them?
Wake up, stop running, stop hiding,
You will never be perfect,
But you'll always flourish,
People will pick you apart and walk over you just to throw
you away as if you never existed,
People are monstrous, always unsatisfied,
The world is cruel, it will always try to hurt you,
It will succeed and it will scar,
These scars will be the key to going far,
Just remember all wounds heal eventually it's how nature
goes.

Lilly Chapman (12)
The Sacred Heart Language College, Wealdstone

Follow Your Dreams

Follow your dreams
they won't be as far as they seem
don't let anything hold you back
from winning that plaque

Follow your dreams
even if you have to do it in teams
do what you think is best
and follow through with that test

Follow your dreams
even though it's through screens
fight for the things you care about
and get through negative thoughts

Follow your dreams
even if people make you scream
be in control of your life
and don't cause a strife

Follow your dreams
let your mind flow
like a stream
be the true king
and queen you are
because a beautiful life
isn't that far.

Marta Sadowska (11)
The Sacred Heart Language College, Wealdstone

My City Has A Lot Of Places

My city has a lot of places,
With murder and crime hidden under people's faces.
As an economy drops,
Pollution pops,
Streets filled with litter,
And weather turning bitter,
Yes, my city has a lot of places.

Mysterious fog hanging in the air,
With extremely frozen weather to bear.
Parks filled with glorious trees,
And extraordinary flowers blossoming in the breeze,
Yes, my city has a lot of places.

Famous monuments visited every day,
And opportunities that make people stay.
Free healthcare all around,
As there are thousands of homeless people in the background,
So yes, my city has a lot of places.

Dália Sequeira (13)
The Sacred Heart Language College, Wealdstone

I Need That Life

Speeding, writing, rushing ahead of time,
I need to have the life that she has,
I love it too much, it must be a crime,
I want the scenery, the music, the jazz,
I feel like a fish on a line.
I need to get good grades or I'll fail,
She's got the husband, the life, she's the bride,
Sitting here while she's sitting in a veil,
Can't sit here and watch, stop trying to hide.
I lie here and feel so frail.
I feel like I'm staring at an exhibition,
Her cherry-red lips, her brown eyes, her smooth skin,
I need to do more to fuel my ambition,
But me being me, I feel I can never win.

Olivia Seah (14)
The Sacred Heart Language College, Wealdstone

Climate Change

C limate change is caused by many different things, people throw their rubbish on the floor and don't think about how it affects our home

L ife could be better if everyone would stop littering

I magine that you lived in a poor country and had no devices, how would you feel if someone was on their phone all day long and you could do nothing about it?

M ake the world better, stop leaving taps on for so long

A void leaving lights open when no one is in the room

T ry to walk, cycle, or take public transport instead of a car

E arth is our common home, do you really want to destroy it?

Isabella Martinas (11)

The Sacred Heart Language College, Wealdstone

I Want To Be Like The Ocean

I think I want to be like the ocean.
I'm almost jealous of it.
The fact that the ocean brims with power and beauty.
The insane amount of mystery it holds,
yet, the delicacy.
I want to be like the ocean.
Or I want to just simply lay down on it,
and just stay there.
Forever and ever, till the confines of time.
I wish I was like the ocean.
Making everybody else feel so little,
but still granting each being new hope.
Sometimes, I feel as if people do not understand,
just how important the ocean really is.
Because if it weren't there, would we be?
I need to be like the ocean.

Raissa Dos Reis Pereira (14)
The Sacred Heart Language College, Wealdstone

Feel, Experience, Think

You can never feel what someone else is feeling
some people hide their bruises by concealing
some feel happy and some feel blue
but you can never tell because you aren't in their shoes

You can never experience what someone else is going
through
not even a clue
people are scared to tell things
maybe because they feel that someone might cut off their
wings

You can never think what someone else is thinking
maybe because you cannot tell whether their eye is
twinkling
you never know what is going on inside someone's brain
because your eyes are surrounded by a metal chain.

Sanvi Vyas (14)
The Sacred Heart Language College, Wealdstone

Don't Worry, It's Okay

You are special, you are unique.
There are many more words that I could pick.
You are something to the world.
We need you, you are amazing.
Don't you worry, so please don't be sorry.
Don't blame yourself, it's not your fault.
You won't get better.

The world is big, it's full of people,
There's going to be someone who you'll tell your favourite riddle,
There will be someone, just take a step forward,
Don't be scared,
Because it won't be awkward.

You have the power,
It's okay,
Because good things will come your way.

Georgia Gennaro (12)
The Sacred Heart Language College, Wealdstone

This Is Me

In the past, it was not up to me
my culture, heritage, or my ethnicity
surrounded by others that weren't like me
I failed to see the power in me

I felt different, like I wasn't free
no power or courage left in me
was this life, it couldn't be

I didn't want to be different
I wanted to be me

My skin was darker
my hair was curlier
my background was different
so, does that define me?

Okay, my hair is different
and I love my curls
just a quick shoutout to all
the black women in the world

Black is beautiful!

Victoria Lubamba (14)
The Sacred Heart Language College, Wealdstone

Meet Me At The Lake

She always loved the water,
The way she felt when she was swimming,
The thrill she got whenever she held her breath,
She was blissful and free.

She loves water, just like her mother did,
She is fourteen and is already the spitting image of her,
She went swimming in the lake near her house and as her
father went to take a call, she dived in.
She was unconscious by the time she reached the bottom.

She used to love water,
If only she knew this would lead to her tragic, untimely
death,
If only she had planned it,
Then she would have been exactly like her mother.

Maxime Dzogang (13)
The Sacred Heart Language College, Wealdstone

Thank You

You gave me a new life
one where I could have fun and not be treated like dice
you helped me find a hidden part of myself
and for that, I want to say thank you

You inspire me to be my best
to try to ignore the world around me, to make me feel less stress
you made the new me, someone fun and loving
and for that, I want to say thank you

Sadly, you moved house, I went back to feeling like no one
bu I'm glad you inspired me to make others feel like someone
even though you made me see who I can be, I miss you, a lot
and for that, I want to say thank you.

Annabelle Do Rosario (11)
The Sacred Heart Language College, Wealdstone

A Girl's Story

When I look in the mirror, I see me,
A young teen who is not sure what she aspires to be,
I see a girl who has many dreams,
A lot of people have interpretations of her,
But she is not who she seems,
When I look in the mirror, I see me,
The girl who tries to put a smile on her face,
But only for everyone else to see,
You would think she's fine when she sits behind you,
But at the back of the class, she is most likely to be breaking
down,
Over the laughter, joys and rumours that are untrue,
The girl, her possible thoughts and her fears, cause her to
drown.

Lydia Daniel Semere (13)
The Sacred Heart Language College, Wealdstone

Talent

A talent is like a sea
A thing which asks us to use it
A thing with which I try to write this poem

Talent, a creative thing in our mind
A thing which helps us do things perfect
To make dreams come true, it's more than enough

We would dance using our talent
We would paint using that
A talent is what everyone has
To make the world creative, colourful, it's more than enough

Talent is a thing we could use any time
A talent is a great gift from God
A talent that makes the world perfect.

Ashley Rose Seby (12)
The Sacred Heart Language College, Wealdstone

Four Walls Choose

One wall, the soul fading away, mentally suffering, not able to leave
Two walls, two tests, waiting for results, positive, again
Three walls, nearly out, chains of isolation, unlocking, nearly off
Four walls, breaking out, crashing through, we can choose
Time ticking and we choose to ignore it, but we should do more
Choose to persevere our world, choose to go to school, choose to wear masks
Test frequently and most of all, care
Stay safe out there
Choose to protect others
Choose four, five, two, one, no more walls.

Olivia Cummings (12)
The Sacred Heart Language College, Wealdstone

My City

In my city, the sky can cry all night,
Another day passes by with rain,
Oh, I wish I could tame,
In my city, the streets are quite busy,
With people scattered in every shop,
The jubilee clock is like our Big Ben and strikes non-stop.

In my city, there are stabbings and crimes,
People are facing death all the time.
There's no peace, no love, no care, just crime.
On November 27th, 2021, a man in his thirties got stabbed.

In my city, some areas are majestic,
And some are not so great.

Heba Hussain (13)
The Sacred Heart Language College, Wealdstone

Stay By My Side

Stay by my side and we'll be here forever,
having fun, always together.
You put a smile on my face every day,
everything we do is play.

Stay by my side and we'll have lots of fun,
baking new things, such as hot cross buns.
Chatting all the time and especially on the way home,
never leaving school with a moan.

Stay by my side, the journey is incomplete,
taking one more step and giving a leap.
You are my one and only best friend,
so, you'll always stay by my side.

Odilia Figueiras (12)
The Sacred Heart Language College, Wealdstone

The Summer Breeze

The summer breeze that makes me sneeze,
but,
it's nothing they can't fix.

The summer breeze and the blossom it brings,
sparks a smile,
it makes me feel alright.

The summer breeze and the birds it brings with all the
buzzing bees,
makes the flowers dance and prance around the new green
leaves.

The summer breeze and the calm it brings me,
makes me want to fly and I can't lie,
when I see the sky,
I say,
I love the summer breeze.

April Tsangaris (13)
The Sacred Heart Language College, Wealdstone

Steps To A Better Environment

E   at healthier and better
N   ever litter or waste
V   ery little time to save our planet
I   ntake, don't overeat and waste
R   emember to save water when you can
O   nly use products that don't test on animals
N   ever take anything for granted
M   aybe try to upcycle things like clothes
E   lectricity, save it when you can
N   ever buy single-use plastic if not needed
T   urn off taps and lights when not in use.

Neneh Dabo (12)
The Sacred Heart Language College, Wealdstone

The Reality Of Life

Deeper insecurities
What if I don't have legacy?
Do you ever fall asleep because you don't want to be awake?
In a way, you're tired of the reality you face
A song without a voice, a spark without a flame
A child without a name, oh, it's just wrong
Like an ocean without a shore
A soldier without a war, how can we do this anymore?
A song without a voice
A spark without a flame
A child without a name
Oh, it's just wrong
The reality of life.

Chloe Caca (12)
The Sacred Heart Language College, Wealdstone

The Place For Me

I wish there was a place to be me
and be free
not a place where I have to be quiet
but a place where I can be seen
not a place where people pretend
because they feel sorry for me
not a place where you're outcasted
because you're small, silent and naive
I want to be in a place for me
where I can be free
where people acknowledge me
and all my wonderful traits
instead of gossiping like loud tweeting birds
and making me feel as lonely as Loki.

Joanne Antony (13)
The Sacred Heart Language College, Wealdstone

My Mother

My mother sacrificed her dreams so I could dream,
Believed in me strengthening my self-esteem,
Spent sleepless nights watching over me,
So, today, I can be who I want to be.

Pushing me up when I go down,
Making me feel like I am the queen to the crown,
Giving me the most unstoppable love,
Covering my cold hand with a glove.

Showing me from the wrong to the right,
To make me feel bright,
Never let me lose hope,
Made sure I went up that rope.

Zainab Tayab (12)
The Sacred Heart Language College, Wealdstone

Freedom, Freedom, Oh Freedom

So many problems, nothing can solve them,
where is this freedom, has it disappeared?
One room only, searching for a puzzle,
matching the ends, so it can all make sense,
positive again, when will this end?
They said two weeks, but it's been two years,
over and over this repeats,
where is this freedom?
Locked up, can't be, how can we end this?
The answers slowly begin to rise as scientists make up their minds,
freedom, freedom,
where did you go?

Giulia Cicu (12)
The Sacred Heart Language College, Wealdstone

Embracing Me

I look in the mirror,
And what do I see,
A young black woman,
Staring back at me.

With dreams and aspirations,
Empowered by females around her,
She's struggled to get to the top,
But hopes that one day the struggle stops.

Her big brown eyes,
Ready to see the world,
Her big voluptuous lips,
Ready to speak her word.

With a spring in her stride,
She steps out to change the world,
One protest at a time.

Noadiah Kennedy (14)
The Sacred Heart Language College, Wealdstone

Dear Past Me

Dear past me,
yes, I cried,
and yes, I lied,
I always thought I would never succeed,
but look at me now.

I have loving friends,
I'm happy,
I finally feel loved,
even though I was sad,
I believed I would succeed.

And guess what?
I did it,
I have good grades,
I even discovered I have hobbies.

Yes, there were bumps across the path,
but I passed them,
it wasn't easy but,
it paid off!

Natalia Gancarczyk (14)
The Sacred Heart Language College, Wealdstone

Take Action Before It's Too Late

Climate change,
Will not help the lane,
But instead, cause pain,
And no more rain.

Do we like nature?
Or do we prefer pollution?
Do not worry,
There is always a solution.

Pollution, pollution, pollution,
You may be unaware of it,
But you are breathing in it.

Love nature,
It is important,
Every part is beautiful,
And we should be delightful,
To have the opportunity,
To see what is rightful.

Andrina Gomes (12)
The Sacred Heart Language College, Wealdstone

The Magic Within Words

Image after image storms into my brain,
As my eyes fill up with words.
I think I have gone insane.
So many ideas start rushing in like herds,
They tend to call us nerds.
But they will never understand the characters like we do,
By reading these words.
We try to say to the author, thank you,
Thank you for creating my world,
Thank you for letting me learn,
Thank you for being there for me,
And thank you for not letting me burn.

Justyna Puterko (13)
The Sacred Heart Language College, Wealdstone

Until We Meet Again, My Old Self

We will meet again
not sure where, not sure when
but I know that we'll meet again, on a lovely day
we'll meet again
not sure why, so I'll try
but I know that we'll meet again on a lovely day
we'll meet again
don't know how, don't feel down
but I know we'll meet again on a lovely day
we'll meet again
if we can't, let's pretend
so, I'll know we'll meet again on a sunny day.

Tobi Kadiri (13)
The Sacred Heart Language College, Wealdstone

My Inspiration

To my inspiration,
I thank you for being here,
Through all my troubles and my fear,
I love you for who you are,
Even though sometimes, you may be far.

To my inspiration,
I thank you for being a friend and a mother,
Always there to be my cover,
Your heart is so warm,
Thank you for me being born.

You have never failed to protect me,
You mean so much more to me than you see,
To my inspiration, thank you.

Thea Porter-German (13)
The Sacred Heart Language College, Wealdstone

Together

You are not alone,
There is someone on the other side of the phone,
They're there to cheer you on,
They are your friend, they will never be gone.

You are not alone,
Have some hope,
Someone has your back, they will help you cope,
Release all of your hatred,
Get help for your trauma and relive the fun memories you've created.

You are not alone,
I am with you,
So, let's get over it, together.

Precious Gbete (12)
The Sacred Heart Language College, Wealdstone

I'm Possible

Impossible is just a word that scares people,
and keeps them in darkness when ahead is dawn,
pulls them back and tears them down,
finishes their dream before they're born,
may have seen yourselves lose,
may not have time to choose.

But, just, it needs a spark of inspiration,
a drop of bravery and a heart full of talent,
to break and tear the word impossible,
and make it into,
I'm possible.

Ahana Das (12)
The Sacred Heart Language College, Wealdstone

An Evacuee

It seems so long ago but the journey has just begun,
I feel really lonely and I'm missing everyone.
A long journey to get here, but it's beginning to feel unclear...
I feel like all my happiness has just disappeared.
Mixed emotions are running through my head,
I don't even know if my family are alive or dead.
I want to go home, I've had enough!
I wish this war could end, it's getting really tough!

Sienna Power (11)
The Sacred Heart Language College, Wealdstone

Who Am I?

Who am I?
What am I?
Why am I?
How am I?
Do I feel unique?
Trying to reach high?
Do I feel special?
Or do I have the courage to lie?
Do I feel like a good person?
Yes, I try and try and try.
Am I just a hopeless person?
Stranded in the middle of a maze?
No, I am me, I am Lujain.
I'm not in a haze or a daze,
I will be the best person,
And so will you, in a second and a gaze.

Lujain Al Awad (12)
The Sacred Heart Language College, Wealdstone

Cloud Of Control

Put your mask on, put your mask on!
Will this ever stop, all these Covid cases?
Rising all around us, loved ones dying and loved ones
mourning.

Global warming slowly rising, people littering all around us,
Will this ever stop?
Animals pleading for their lives,
Knowing that they might not survive.

Will this ever stop?
Will the world be the same?
Will we ever see the world as we used to?

Melanie Shaikh (12)
The Sacred Heart Language College, Wealdstone

Today

Stand up strong and say what you believe
Speak with power today but never aspire to be sour, no way
Keep your chin up high today, while your imagination starts
to fly away
Embrace your responsibility today, live with no regrets today
Dream to be you, as that is all you can do today
Make a change today, in a unique way
Because today is your day
Everything you change today, you will aspire to change
every day.

Molly Carey (12)
The Sacred Heart Language College, Wealdstone

Imagine

Imagine if all your dreams came true
What would you feel like?
What would you do?

Imagine you're a bird, soaring through the air
With the wind in your face
But you wouldn't care

You are flying high into the sky
And every breath you take
Is a memory you make

Imagine you are happy, happy for evermore
With your family and friends
And nothing more to wish for!

Gabriella Cameron (11)
The Sacred Heart Language College, Wealdstone

Myself

I've always been a big fan of reading
It has always helped me think of better versions of myself
I imagine myself being very confident, like the main characters
I imagine myself being a colourful dragon that's filled with might
And that can all happen in reality
I know that I can be confident and full of might
Anyone can be confident if they believe in themselves
Like I believe in myself.

Victoria Damian (11)
The Sacred Heart Language College, Wealdstone

Be You

Y ou are amazing just the way you are

O utside your heart, there might be insecurities, but don't push it too far

U nder all that sadness, there is always a spark of happiness

R emember who you are, a wonderful human being

S ee who you can be, be you

E veryone should know who you are, do you

L ove yourself, love others

F irst of all, love you.

Vishalini Ponnuthurai (11)
The Sacred Heart Language College, Wealdstone

Listen To Me

Listen to me
you can change this world
one step at a time

Listen to me
you can change yourself for the greater good
one step at a time

Listen to me
life is shorter than it seems, so make the most of it
one step at a time

Last time I ask, but please listen to me
you're in charge of a world given to us by God
please fix it, one step at a time.

Rheya-Leigh Sturridge (11)
The Sacred Heart Language College, Wealdstone

Friendship

Someone who will care for you
Someone who will stay with you
We have fun together
We help each other
But not everyone is that good
Some of them are bad but feel cool
They used to bully you and break your friendship
Only a true friend would continue this friendship
Go play and chat with your friends
Go have fun and enjoy with them
If she's really a true friend.

Natalie Hui (11)
The Sacred Heart Language College, Wealdstone

Apple Pie

The sweet aroma grounds me in my place,
it smells so beautiful and all I want is a taste,
I'd take it anywhere with me, to space,
the taste so divine at the tip of my tongue,
this is the prize that is a victory once I've won,
the sweet aroma of apple pie, just like the one
the one that I've known since I was young
it takes me back to the place from where I had begun.

Natalia Gancarczyk (14)
The Sacred Heart Language College, Wealdstone

The Future

Dear future self,
A quick reminder to continue working on your health
And don't be afraid to admit how you feel
Not like what you see on an Instagram reel
It is okay to keep at your own pace
Life ain't a race
Remember, to keep your head up high
Right up to the sky

Dear future me,
Float like a wasp, sting like a bee
You can finally be free.

Kenechi Ezeajughi (13)
The Sacred Heart Language College, Wealdstone

Person I Will Never Forget

You give me life, you give me happiness
You help me when I need it
And for that, I say thank you

You gave me love
You gave me power
You gave me strength
And for that, I want to say how grateful I am

You held my hand, you gave me confidence
For that, I want to say how I feel
You remind me who I am and for that, I say
I love you.

Anne Shelton (11)
The Sacred Heart Language College, Wealdstone

Football Fun

Football is great,
I play it with my mates,
The determination to get the win,
The pain when you lose feels like being dropped like a pin.
The tackles are hard,
But we are enough,
The kick of the ball,
The hurt of the fall,
The race against time,
That goal is mine,
Win after win,
Loss after loss,
We still power through the game!

Kate Gurhy (12)
The Sacred Heart Language College, Wealdstone

Seasons

A shadow of hard stone
Shivers in the soft water
Icy water nights

A breath of fresh air
The explosion of sight, sound and colour
Spring, the poetry of nature

The smell of saltwater
White sand, hot under my feet
A gleaming pink shell

Red and brown leaves falling
Muddy fields all across
Autumn has arrived.

Riana Antonia Petrisor (12)
The Sacred Heart Language College, Wealdstone

Choose

I have a choice, whenever to use my voice,
For good or bad, to be happy, to be sad,
I can be foe or friend, attack or defend,
Be a follower or lead, starve them or feed,
I can be idle or learn, show hate or concern,
It's my choice to decide if I win or lose,
Take the right road or wrong,
It's my life, it's my song.

Amy Flynn (12)
The Sacred Heart Language College, Wealdstone

Stop!

Stop, before it's too late,
Stop, take care of the Earth that God made,
Stop, help all the animals that are dying,
Stop, help those that are crying,
Stop, help animals that are being abused,
Stop, spread the news,
Stop, be positive and kind,
Stop, this is our world we are ruining,
Act before it's too late.

Kaitlyn Joyce (11)
The Sacred Heart Language College, Wealdstone

About My Friends

To my best friend
Hope you're doing well
Just know that
I'm here for you
And life is swell

To my best friend
Promise me you won't forget
Our laughs, tears
And when I fed your pet

To my best friend
Please remember me
When you go off
Chasing your dreams.

Eugenie Malvezin (11)
The Sacred Heart Language College, Wealdstone

Drowned Land

Drowned land,
The flowers start to sink,
Drowned land,
The hedges start to shrink,

Drowned land,
The writing fades away,
Drowned land,
The moss takes over the stone every day,

Drowned land,
That will change,
Drowned land,
Let's hope the sun can reach this range.

Jade Montes (13)
The Sacred Heart Language College, Wealdstone

One Step

One step to reach your goals
to succeed, to believe
one step live life freely
to never worry, to never feel held back.

One step to love yourself
to never change, to be you
one step to be happy
to be proud, to be loud.

One step to be on top
to be number one
one more hop.

Julia Kucia (12)
The Sacred Heart Language College, Wealdstone

Power Is Change

P atiently waiting for someone to speak up is not power
O beying people can sometimes take over
W aiting won't change things now
E specially when things need to change
R ight now is present, tomorrow is the future and we need
  to think in the present and change in the future.

Colette Grant (11)
The Sacred Heart Language College, Wealdstone

Our Earth Is Slowly Dying

When will we stop? Our Earth is beginning to rot.
Our animals are dying and sea levels are rising.
But have we stopped?
We have nowhere else to go,
So why are we getting our future kids and relatives
involved?
We need to act now, before it's too late,
Before we regret all of our mistakes.

Raya Georgieva (11)
The Sacred Heart Language College, Wealdstone

If You're Asking

If you're asking, if I need you
then, the answer is forever
If you're asking if I'll ever leave you
the answer is never
If you're asking what do I value
The answer is you
If you're asking if I love you
The answer is yes I do
very much I do.

Tatiana Soares De Graca (12)
The Sacred Heart Language College, Wealdstone

I Am What I Am

I stand out from the crowd
I am bold
I am compassionate
I am valued
I am considerate
I am intelligent
I am deserved
I am equal
I am loyal
I am safe
And I am loved.

Vailanni Peixoto (11)
The Sacred Heart Language College, Wealdstone

Reality

I see myself
Riding a white mustang against the never-ending sands
The gentle current pushing us to the luscious lands
The stallion's hooves one by one, disappearing through the
golden beads
Away from the city's speed
Whilst behind my back, I stare at glimpsing sunrise
Stepping forward on the amber skies
The ocean waves singing with the air
Whilst I ride with a graceful flare
But in reality, I sit at the back of the class
Staring out of the window glass
All I hear is the rain tapping against the windowpane
As I stare at the cars passing through the lane
Life rolls faster and faster every day
And when I go home, I think about everything as I lay.

Zuzanna Filipczyk (11)
West Buckland School, Barnstaple

Strength

Strength has powerful people,
Strength has powerful things,
Strength has a powerful meaning with all the strength it
brings,
People live across the globe, with their friends and family,
Looking out for each other, in peace and harmony,
Life has powerful people, life has powerful things,
Life has a powerful meaning,
With all the strength it brings,
People believe in different things,
Like we were made by gods,
Some believe a bang occurred,
How are we to know?
People have power,
People have strength,
People are important,
With all the strength they bring.

Emily Goddard (11)
West Buckland School, Barnstaple

YOUNG WRITERS INFORMATION

We hope you have enjoyed reading this book – and that you will continue to in the coming years.

If you're the parent or family member of an enthusiastic poet or story writer, do visit our website **www.youngwriters.co.uk/subscribe** and sign up to receive news, competitions, writing challenges and tips, activities and much, much more! There's lots to keep budding writers motivated!

If you would like to order further copies of this book, or any of our other titles, then please give us a call or order via your online account.

Young Writers
Remus House
Coltsfoot Drive
Peterborough
PE2 9BF
(01733) 890066
info@youngwriters.co.uk

Join in the conversation!
Tips, news, giveaways and much more!

 YoungWritersUK 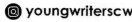 YoungWritersCW  youngwriterscw